Pulleys

Andrea Rivera

abdopublishing.com

Published by Abdo Zoom™, PO Box 398166, Minneapolis, Minnesota 55439. Copyright © 2017 by Abdo Consulting Group, Inc. International copyrights reserved in all countries. No part of this book may be reproduced in any form without written permission from the publisher. Abdo Zoom™ is a trademark and logo of Abdo Consulting Group, Inc.

Printed in the United States of America, North Mankato, Minnesota
102016
012017

THIS BOOK CONTAINS RECYCLED MATERIALS

Cover Photo: Poul Riishede/iStockphoto
Interior Photos: Poul Riishede/iStockphoto, 1; iStockphoto, 4, 6, 7, 9, 14, 15; Bob Balestri/iStockphoto, 5; Shutterstock Images, 8, 10, 11, 18, 21; Kyoungil Jeon/iStockphoto, 13; Martin Mojzis/Shutterstock Images, 16–17

Editor: Brienna Rossiter
Series Designer: Madeline Berger
Art Direction: Dorothy Toth

Publisher's Cataloging-in-Publication Data
Names: Rivera, Andrea, author.
Title: Pulleys / by Andrea Rivera.
Description: Minneapolis, MN : Abdo Zoom, 2017. | Series: Simple machines | Includes bibliographical references and index.
Identifiers: LCCN 2016949160 | ISBN 9781680799545 (lib. bdg.) | ISBN 9781624025402 (ebook) | ISBN 9781624025969 (Read-to-me ebook)
Subjects: LCSH: Pulleys--Juvenile literature.
Classification: DDC 621.8--dc23
LC record available at http://lccn.loc.gov/2016949160

Table of Contents

Science 4

Technology. 8

Engineering 10

Art 14

Math 16

Key Stats. 20

Glossary 22

Booklinks 23

Index 24

Science

Pulleys are **simple machines**.

The parts of a pulley work together to lift things. A pulley makes a **load** feel lighter. Less **force** is needed to lift a load.

Pulleys have a wheel. The wheel has a **groove**.

A rope or chain goes inside the groove. It helps to move the load.

Technology

Pulleys give a **mechanical advantage**.

The load is on one end of the rope.
A person pulls on the other end.
This moves the load.

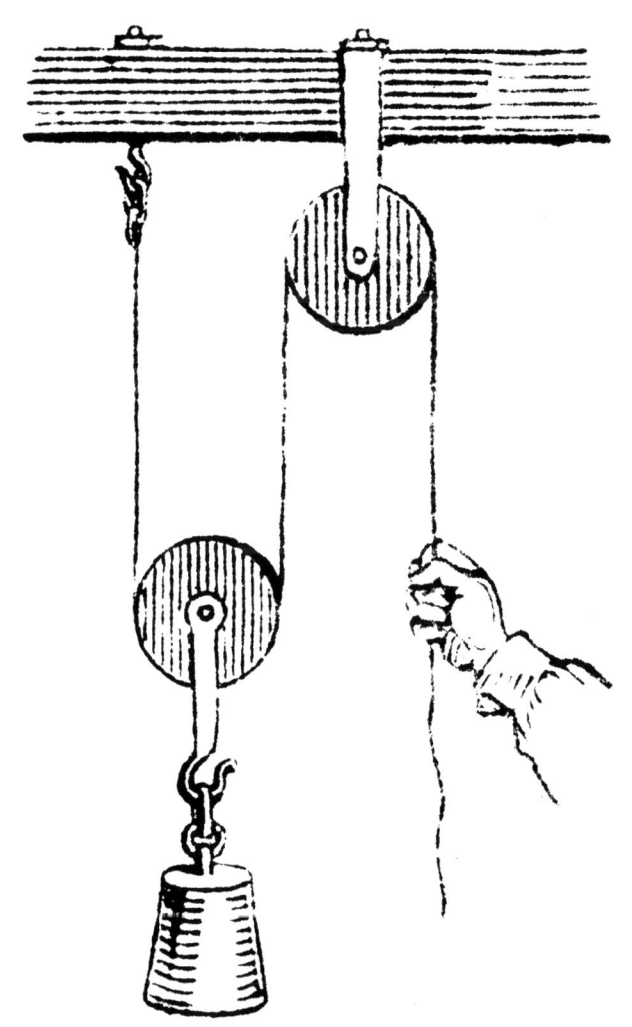

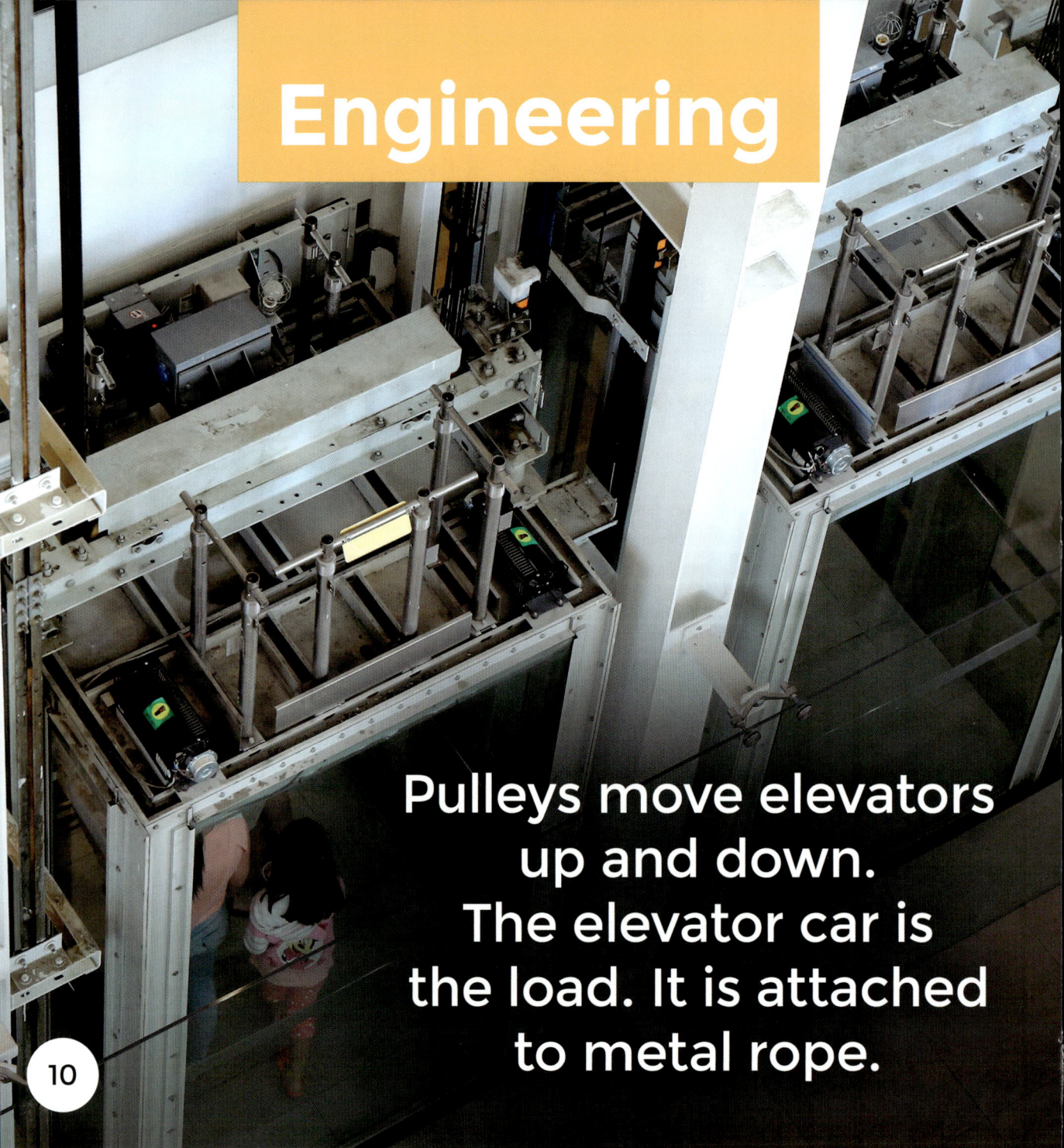

Engineering

Pulleys move elevators up and down. The elevator car is the load. It is attached to metal rope.

The rope rests in the groove of a wheel.

A motor provides the force. This lifts and lowers the elevator.

Art

Most flagpoles use pulleys.

They help raise and lower the flag.
Each country has its own flag.
They have different designs.

Math

Very heavy loads need a compound pulley.

It has more than one pulley. The pulleys work together to lift the load.

Each additional pulley makes the load feel lighter.

Using three pulleys makes the load feel lighter than using just two pulleys.

- Fishing poles use pulleys. The pulleys make it easier to reel in a heavy fish.

- Cranes are pulleys. They lift heavy loads in construction sites.

- Some rock climbers use pulleys to climb or lift equipment.

- Sailors use pulleys. They raise and lower the sails of a ship.

- Window blinds use pulleys. They raise and lower the blinds.

Glossary

force - a push or pull that causes a change in motion.

groove - a long, narrow channel cut into something.

load - an object that needs to be turned, lifted, or moved.

mechanical advantage - the way a simple machine makes work easier.

simple machine - a basic device that makes work easier.

Booklinks

For more information on **pulleys**, please visit booklinks.abdopublishing.com

 In on STEAM!

Learn even more with the Abdo Zoom STEAM database. Check out **abdozoom.com** for more information.

Index

compound pulley, 16

elevators, 10, 12

flagpoles, 14

force, 5, 12

groove, 6, 7, 11

lift, 5, 12, 17

load, 5, 7, 9, 10, 16, 17, 18, 19

mechanical advantage, 8

rope, 7, 9, 10, 11

simple machines, 4

wheel, 6, 11